BRIEF LESSONS IN

Creativity

...published in the United Kingdom in 2019 by Ilex, an imprint of Octopus Publishing Group Ltd
Carmelite House
50 Victoria Embankment
London EC4Y 0DZ
www.octopusbooks.co.uk
www.octopusbooksusa.com

Distributed in the US by
Hachette Book Group
1290 Avenue of the Americas
4th and 5th Floors
New York, NY 10104

Distributed in Canada by
Canadian Manda Group
664 Annette St.
Toronto, Ontario, Canada M6S 2C8

Publisher: Alison Starling
Commissioning Editor: Zara Anvari
Managing Editor: Rachel Silverlight
Editor: Jenny Dye
Art Director: Ben Gardiner
Designer: Luke Bird
Production Manager: Caroline Alberti

Ilex are proud to partner with Tate in our publishing programme; supporting the gallery in its mission to promote public understanding and enjoyment of British, modern and contemporary art.

Frances Ambler asserts the moral right to be identified as the author of this work.

ISBN 978-1-78157-671-7

A CIP catalogue record for this book is available from the British Library.

Printed and bound in the UK

10 9 8 7 6 5 4 3 2 1

BRIEF LESSONS IN
CREATIVITY

FRANCES AMBLER

ilex

CONTENTS

Introduction

Delve into the minds of some of history's most creative figures. These are the people whose inventiveness has changed the course of art. It's not only the work of these influencers that continues to inspire; their methods also offer valuable lessons to anyone who aspires to follow in their footsteps.

Take a closer look at these creative masterminds. Learn to see the world afresh through their unique ways of looking; discover, from their processes, practical ideas for reinvigorating your work.

* Find out how to get started with Paul Klee and Tacita Dean.
* Become seriously curious, just like Robert Rauschenberg.
* Understand why Paul Cézanne and David Hockney are so fond of repeating themselves.
* Let Joan Jonas show you how to get moving to boost your creativity.
* Learn to improvise, guided by Alberto Giacometti and Rebecca Warren.
* Follow the example of Francis Bacon and get inspired by what's around you – or, like Carolee Schneemann, simply use yourself.
* Try a hands-on approach, like Henri Matisse and Grayson Perry.
* Discover why Lucian Freud and Agnes Martin were so insistent on having their own space, and why you should be, too.

Think of this as an ideas blueprint – a guide to creating great things. Keep it in your pocket, ready for when you want fresh eyes on a challenging problem or need to banish creative block. Use smart thinking from these innovative minds to generate better ideas more frequently, and to aid you in nurturing and sustaining your creativity. The results can be life-changing.

TACITA DEAN
EVA HESSE
PAUL KLEE

Pick up a pencil, pick up a paintbrush, scribble, scrawl, splash. START. There are hundreds of ways to begin – so why don't we? This simple action gets diluted by a multitude of feelings – insecurities, doubts, fear – that can hold us back from simply doing. American artist Sol LeWitt was well aware of this in 1965, when he wrote to fellow artist Eva Hesse offering advice as universal as it is heartfelt, in what has become one of the most famous letters about creative block: 'Just stop thinking, worrying, looking over your shoulder, wondering, doubting, fearing, hurting, hoping for some easy way out', he told her. 'Stop it, and just do.'[1]

DO BEGIN SOMEWHERE

In the words of Pablo Picasso: 'To know what you're going to draw, you have to begin drawing.'[2] The start of something new, when you are full of ambitions for what you want to achieve, is exciting, but that kind of big thinking can also be terrifying. Start in a small way. Look at what's in front of you and do something with it, even if it seems unpromising. Painter Chris Ofili starts work each day by tearing up a sheet of paper – always the same size – into eight pieces, which he then marks with his pencil. 'They're not a guide,' he says, 'they're just a way to say something and nothing with a physical mark.'[3] He sets the pieces aside and moves on to his main project. Ofili reaps the benefits of an established routine – consider creating your own ritual if you find getting started a challenge. ✱

Another way of starting was suggested by the artist Paul Klee in his *Pädagogisches Skizzenbuch* (*Pedagogical Sketchbook*, 1925, first translated into English by Sibyl Moholy-Nagy in 1953). This manual was based on classes the artist taught at the famous Bauhaus art school in Germany. He showed how to begin with the simplest of marks and build from there. With his famous idea of 'an active line on a walk', Klee shows

✱ ——— MAKE SPACE (see p.38)

the many directions in which a simple line can be taken and describes this process as a way of seeing the world.[4] It was an exercise that didn't even need a purpose: it could simply be 'a walk for a walk's sake'.[5]

You can see this idea put into motion in Klee's 1927 painting *Ships in the Dark* (see page 97). The rocking ships echo a diagram in his *Sketchbook*, showing 'an active line, limited in its movement by fixed points'.[6] In another work of that year, *Portrait of an Equilibrist*, Klee references his diagram showing a tightrope walker with a bamboo pole. When stalled or overwhelmed, it's always worth going back to the line. Try continuous line drawing to loosen up hand and mind. Klee used this technique in works such as *Girl with Doll Carriage* (1930), while Picasso so enjoyed making his 'one liners' he used them to depict a host of motifs ranging from harlequins to centaurs, and ringmasters to sausage dogs.

DO THIS

Grab a pen or pencil and some paper. You can't take the pen or pencil off the paper until your drawing is finished. Pick your subject, put your nib to the paper and go! Concentrate on the process over the result. There's no stopping to rub out, but you can overlap lines and experiment with thinner or thicker strokes. Discover what your tools can do within these limits. Stuck for inspiration? Try the surrealist technique of automatic drawing. Trace your pen across the page without any control or preconceived notions of what you are trying to draw. Only lift the pen from the paper when you feel like you are 'done'.

For Klee, a line taken for a walk was also a metaphor for expressing metaphysical and spiritual ideas. Stanley William Hayter, a painter and printmaker, described how Klee made suggestions 'which you could follow and go farther with, which would challenge you and propose things to you'.[7] Hayter promoted Klee's theories to artists such as Jackson Pollock and Robert Motherwell. In Klee, these figures saw an emphasis on process – the simple act of doing – and from there, took his line to places that Klee himself would never have dreamed of.

In fact, there's an active line of influence that can be traced from Klee to Eva Hesse. At the Yale School of Art and Architecture, Hesse studied under Josef Albers, once Klee's student and later his colleague at the Bauhaus. Albers had absorbed lessons from Klee and incorporated them into his own teachings, in turn passing them on to his students in the United States. LeWitt's letter, quoted on page 9, arrived towards the end of a later, year-long residency in Germany. It was one of the prompts she needed to put everything that she had learned into practice – to push through her struggles and simply do. ✱ She began her year drawing images of intricate and interlinked machines; she finished it with a much bolder, looser style. As described by art historian Ellen H. Johnson, Hesse's line 'finally…flowed off its support into real space'.[8] She also began to create work in three dimensions, leading on to the organic sculptures, made from unconventional materials, for which she is renowned. Hesse had taken the line for a walk.

✱
↓
MAKE IT UP AS YOU GO ALONG (see p.58)

FOLLOW THE THREAD

'Doing' doesn't always have to be physical – you can also let your mind go for a walk. This is a process that shapes the art of English artist Tacita Dean. Works she admires are those in which the artist had 'no real sense of their destination when they started'.[9]

Dean is constantly amassing source material: finding vintage postcards and photographs in street markets, adding to her collection of four-leaf clovers, reading, and shooting far more film than will ever make it into her finished work. ✱ From this abundance of material, her subjects emerge. She is searching for 'that tiny thread to get myself going'.[10]

Dean's 2006 work *Majesty* (see pages 98–9) is an enlarged and over-painted photograph of one of the oldest oak trees in England. The thread that took Dean here begins with a postcard found in Japan, which led her to the Forest of Fontainebleau in France, and then on to the ancient

✱ —→ COLLECT, RECOLLECT (see p.48)

Fredville Oak, situated not far from where Dean grew up in Kent. Her process, she says, is similar to that of the writer W. G. Sebald – it is like a dog, crossing a field, following its nose. Another work in the same series, depicting an ancient tree known as the Crowhurst Yew, shares its name with one of Dean's frequent subjects: Donald Crowhurst, a sailor who disappeared at sea. The Crowhurst link was entirely coincidental, as often occurs in Dean's work. 'I think that being very open to coincidences, they happen more', she says.[11]

The demands of everyday life can make it hard to chance upon such possibilities. The following exercise is like a scavenger hunt, and gives you a way of tuning into the world around you. ✱ Give it a go – who knows what treasures it will help you discover along the way.

✱
⟶
CURIOUSER & CURIOUSER (see p.18)

SNAP

Each day for ten days, head out for a walk. As you're walking, collect something that interests you, such as a stone, a leaf or an object that's been discarded on the street. Your challenge for the walk back on each day is to find another item that matches the first one in some way: in colour, size, material or name, for example. You can repeat objects over the ten days but you can't repeat similar links. Record your findings every day: what you picked up, how and when. Describe what drew you to each object.

At the end of the period, gather together all the material and your notes. What do they tell you as a group, and as visual objects? How do they function as a record of your last ten days?

DEVELOP A
MINDSET
OF NOT
MINDING

Following a thread doesn't always bring results – for Dean, it has often led to a dead end: 'and that is the terrifying part'.[12] It is also a lengthy process: Dean's 2018 film, *Antigone* – combining Greek mythology, landscapes from Yellowstone National Park in North America to Cornwall's Bodmin Moor, the solar eclipse and much more – was her 'unmade project for 20 years'.[13] Works such as these are created from persistence, a refusal to drop the thread despite uncertainty about where it leads.

Antigone is also about blindness, a state Dean seeks in her own method: 'I just try and pursue blindness at all costs,' she says.[14] Embracing the unknown and surrendering to the process of doing appear in LeWitt's advice to Hesse: 'But when you work or before your work you have to empty your mind and concentrate on what you are doing.'[15] Dean, Klee and LeWitt value the creativity that comes from trusting in the process of doing. They also remain open to possibilities, rather than the practice of sticking to a predetermined path. Look at Klee's active line. It's taking 'a walk for a walk's sake' – it is 'moving freely, without goal'.[16] Don't think about it too much. Just do.

★ —→ MAKE IT UP AS YOU GO ALONG (see p.58)

See this:

Tacita Dean, *Majesty,* **2006**

A chain of coincidences ended with this imposing work, 3-metres (9.8-feet) tall and over 4-metres (13-feet) wide.

Eva Hesse, *Tomorrow's Apples (5 in White),* **1965**

Hesse starts taking the line for a walk, experimenting with making reliefs.

Paul Klee, *Ships in the Dark,* **1927**

Klee puts his theory into motion.

Notes 1. Quoted in Shaun Usher (ed.), *Letters of Note: Correspondence Deserving of a Wider Audience* (Edinburgh: Canongate, 2013), p.88   2. Quoted in Brassaï, *Conversations with Picasso,* tr. Jane Marie Todd (Chicago: London: University of Chicago Press, 2002), p.66   3. Quoted in Michael Kimmelman, 'Wake Up. Wash Face. Do Routine. Now Paint'. https://www. nytimes.com/2005/05/08/arts/design/wake-up-wash-face-do-routine-now-paint.html <8 May 2005 (accessed 19 September 2018)>   4. Paul Klee, *Pedagogical Sketchbook* (New York: Praeger Publishers, 1972 [1953]). p.16   5. Ibid.   6. Ibid., p.18   7. Quoted in Carolyn Lanchner, with Paul-Klee-Stiftung, Kunstmuseum Bern, *Paul Klee: His Life and Work* (New York: Hatje Cantz, 2001), p.104   8. Ellen H. Johnson, *Eva Hesse: A Retrospective of the Drawings,* exh. cat., (Oberlin, Ohio: Allen Memorial Art Museum, 1982). p.17   9. Quoted in 'Tacita Dean by Jeffrey Eugenides', *BOMB* 95. Spring 2006, pp.30–7   10. Quoted ibid.   11. Quoted ibid.   12. Quoted in Tim Adams, 'Tacita Dean: The Acclaimed Artist Poised to Make History', https:// www.theguardian.com/artanddesign/2018/mar/11/tacita-dean-interview-celluloid-heroine-london-exhibitions-film <11 March 2018 (accessed 19 September 2018)>   13. Quoted in Louisa Buck, 'Tacita Dean on her Three Major London Shows'. https://www.theartnewspaper. com/interview/genre-fluidity-tacita-dean-on-her-three-london-shows   <13   March   2018 (accessed 19 September 2018)>   14. Quoted in Adams   15. Usher, p.90   16. Klee. p.16

CURIOUSER
&
CURIOUSER

RICHARD LONG
HELEN MARTEN
ROBERT RAUSCHENBERG

For creativity, it pays to be a bit more like Leonardo da Vinci. 'If you look upon an old wall covered with dirt, or the odd appearance of some streaked stones,' he said, 'you may discover several things like landscapes, battles, clouds, uncommon attitudes, humorous faces, draperies, etc. Out of this confused mass of objects, the mind will be furnished with abundance of designs and subjects perfectly new.'[1] Leonardo's advice, to seek inspiration everywhere, is just as applicable five centuries later. Like him, perhaps you too can conjure new designs from dirt or fresh subjects from humble stones if you're open to such possibilities. Or to put it a different way: how interesting can your work be if you're not interested in the world around you?

TRY
THIS
NOT
THAT

Curiosity is a defining characteristic of many celebrated artists. Look at Robert Rauschenberg who was curious about everything, from dance to science, and not least about what art could be. He echoed Leonardo in his suggestion 'I think that I can use ideas of any sort as an excuse to begin working.'[2] The proof can be seen in his output, which made creative use of materials not usually considered art supplies, including windows, Coca-Cola bottles, stuffed goats and even a vat of bubbling mud.

NATURAL
SELECTION

Create a piece of art using only natural materials that you have collected. Be as imaginative as you can: build structures from pine cones, sew leaves together, use the texture of wood to print, try applying paint with a stone. Explore the qualities of each material as if it's a new tool that you're experiencing for the first time. Just play around and ignore the pressure to be perfect.

Art like Rauschenberg's is based on posing questions. 'How about?' and 'what if?' are essential lines of enquiry for any artist. Rauschenberg used them to create new opportunities – looking back over his career, he noted: 'Nearly everything that I've done was to see what would happen if I did this instead of that.'[3]

ENJOY
FINDING
THINGS OUT

Explore as widely and as passionately as possible. Helen Marten is one of the many artists inspired by Rauschenberg. Her complex assemblages appear to bring together found objects. Look closer and you'll see many have been handcrafted from other materials – a rubber 'sock' for example. As in Rauschenberg's pieces, Marten's work may encompass materials not usually considered destined for art – *Becoming Branch* (2014), for instance, includes airbrushed wood, a truck tyre and a tree stump. But before Marten begins 'anything tangible or physical',[4] she deliberately immerses herself in research, spending three or four months reading across genres without 'a specific end goal in mind'.[5] For artists, indulging your curiosity isn't really indulgence – it's a necessity. When you plan your day, mark out blocks of time for research, as well as for making. Allow yourself distraction-free thinking time. ✱

✱
|
↓
MAKE SPACE (see p.38)

As a creator, it pays to know your art history, as well as what's going on in the art world right now. Even more crucial, however, is to look beyond that, at the things that capture your attention and that your fellow artists aren't delving into. Grayson Perry recommends not dismissing 'silly ideas', because 'coolness is the enemy of creativity. Do pay attention to the things that hipsters haven't noticed yet.'[6] Look to what you are enthusiastic about, rather than everyone else's enthusiasms.

Think of the 16th-century *wunderkammern* – the cabinets of curiosities that preceded museums. Intended to act as microcosms of the known world, these not only displayed works of art, but also finds from nature, including geological, ethnographic and archaeological specimens, blurring the boundaries – as we've since been taught to see them – between art and science. Look to other disciplines to make 'art' – there's a whole world of wonder to explore. Embrace the spirit of physicist Richard P. Feynman who, in *The Pleasure of Finding Things Out*, advised, 'Study hard what interests you the most in the most undisciplined, irreverent and original manner possible.'[7] Rauschenberg explored music and dance, experimenting with his contemporaries, the choreographer Merce Cunningham and composer John Cage. In the mid-1960s, he co-founded Experiments in Art and Technology (EAT) to encourage collaboration between engineers and artists and to merge the two titular disciplines. He believed in sharing ideas and experiences, unafraid of asking others to help bridge the gaps in his own knowledge. You don't have to be a lone adventurer.

LOOK

AROUND YOU

★ ⟶ ↓ KEEP ON MOVING (see p.66)

Be curious about your surroundings. The streets emerge as inspiration in the work of both Rauschenberg and Marten – a modern application of Leonardo's advice. Marten says that the city – in her case, London – and the objects, substances and people that move in and out of it are catalysts for her work. Each walk on its streets offers new insights, she says, 'like unfolding a love letter'.[8]

For Rauschenberg, the city literally provided his raw material. When he felt his work was missing something, he simply went out and walked his New York block to find it. The painting *Allegory* (1959–60), for example, features a piece of crumpled tin, found as the result of 'bulldozers' work in tearing down a building in the neighbourhood'.[9] The artist relished the possibility of encountering the unknown. 'There was real adventure about just knowing that you need something in order to make something out of and just looking around and seeing what there was.'[10]

★★ ⟶ ↓ MAKE IT UP AS YOU GO ALONG (see p.58)

Both artists chose to immerse themselves in their surroundings rather than simply move through them. It's a tactic that's easily replicated – take yourself for a walk wherever you are. Leave your phone and headphones at home. ★ Landscape artist Richard Long's work is based on the experience of taking solitary walks all over the world. His love of being in the landscape began as a child when he was using the countryside around Bristol as his 'childhood playground'.[11] His work uses traces of his movements within the landscape, as in *A Line Made by Walking* (1967) (see pages 100–1), or gentle rearrangements of natural materials, either in situ or transported to a gallery. They range in scale, 'from a fingerprint to a thousand miles'.[12] His art is embedded in the landscape as he walks it, and its making is entirely dependent on what he might find in that moment. 'I rely to a degree on intuition and chance,' he says.[13] ★★ Like Rauschenberg, he believes it's about going 'out into the world with an open mind'.[14] Curiosity isn't static. As the British painter and printmaker Tess Jaray explains, 'It is life itself, not the "art world", that is the springboard for the work.'[15] Let yourself be open to life; try things out; really pay attention to what's happening around you.

LOOKING WITH AN OPEN MIND

This exercise is about tuning into your surroundings – trying to look with the same open mind that characterises the work of Long and Rauschenberg. It can be done anywhere, but would work well somewhere like a coffee shop, train station or even a train carriage. You're going to spend about two hours in that space, looking closely and recording your observations through notes and sketches. What does the space look like – what are its colours, textures, shapes? Are there posters or signs? How do other people use the space?

Note how they move through it, where they pause, where they sit, how long they stay. Record the sounds of the place; make a note of snippets of overheard conversations. What does it smell (and taste) like? Change your position within the space at least once. Once you've left, distil your observations into a guide for someone else: it could be a map, or perhaps even a diagram of the space. Fill it with the details you think are the most important – a snapshot of what it felt like to be in that space in that particular moment in time.

COLLECT, RECOLLECT (see p.48)

Ways of 'collecting' and using what inspires you are mentioned later in this book. For now, however, forget about the practicalities. Try to imagine looking at the world as you might if you were a child. Then, try that again through the viewpoint of someone else – a friend, someone in your family, perhaps even Rauschenberg himself. How would you see things differently? As Long says, 'despite the many traditions of walking – the landscape walker, the walking poet, the pilgrim – it is always possible to walk in new ways'.[16] It's a process that should be as fun and joyful as it is productive. And it's not just beneficial to your creativity, but also to the way you live your life. In the words of David Hockney: 'If you see the world as beautiful, thrilling and mysterious, as I think I do, then you feel quite alive.'[17]

See this:

Richard Long, *A Line Made by Walking*, 1967

A formative work: the photograph is a record of the art – Long's intervention in the landscape.

Robert Rauschenberg, *N.Y.C. (Stop)*, 1951, printed 1979

Photography was important to Rauschenberg throughout his career. This is from a series of 12 prints depicting everyday life in New York.

Notes 1. Quoted in James Cahill, *Ways of Being: Advice for Artists by Artists* (London: Laurence King, 2018), p.135 2. Quoted in David Sylvester, *Interviews with American Artists* (London: Chatto & Windus, 2001), p.137 3. Quoted in Sam Hunter, *Robert Rauschenberg: Works, Writings and Interviews* (Barcelona: Polígrafa, 2006) p.134 4. Quoted in Charlotte Higgins, 'Helen Marten: From a Macclesfield Garage to Artist of the Year', https://www.theguardian.com/artanddesign/2016/nov/22/helen-marten-from-a-macclesfield-garage-to-artist-of-the-year <22 November 2016 (accessed 16 September 2018)> 5. Quoted ibid. 6. Quoted in Sarah Thornton, *33 Artists in 3 Acts* (London: Granta, 2015), p.309 7. Quoted in Brian Dillon, *Curiosity: Art and the Pleasures of Knowing* (London: Hayward Publishing, 2013), p.221 8. Quoted in Hannah Ellis-Petersen, 'Helen Marten: The Turner Prize Winner Who Took the Art World to Task', https://www.theguardian.com/artanddesign/2016/dec/09/helen-marten-turner-prize-winner-art-world <9 December 2016 (accessed 16 September 2018)> 9. Quoted in Sylvester, p.135 10. Quoted in Leah Dickerman and Achim Borchardt-Hume (eds), *Robert Rauschenberg* (London: Tate Publishing, 2016), p.18 11. Quoted in William Cook, 'I Walk the Line: How Richard Long Turns Epic Journeys into Art', http://www.bbc.co.uk/programmes/articles/1lwlwQLyGK4FR0lTPTkIBh9/i-walk-the-line-how-richard-long-turns-epic-journeys-into-art, <10 May 2018 (accessed 28 September 2018)> 12. Quoted ibid. 13. Quoted in Sean O'Hagan, 'One Step Beyond', https://www.theguardian.com/artanddesign/2009/may/10/art-richard-long <10 May 2008 (accessed 28 September 2018)> 14. Quoted ibid. 15. Quoted in Cahill, p.89 16. Quoted in O'Hagan 17. Quoted in Nikos Stangos (ed.), *That's The Way I See It: David Hockney* (London: Thames & Hudson, 1993), p.164

REPEAT

REPEAT

REPEAT

PAUL CÉZANNE
DAVID HOCKNEY

As well as doing, artists need to look and practise a kind of looking that is sustained and repeated. Think of Claude Monet, who turned his attention again and again to water lilies, haystacks and cathedrals, and French post-impressionist Paul Cézanne, who painted Provençal landmark Montagne Sainte-Victoire over 60 times (see pages 102–3). Think also of Katsushika Hokusai's *Thirty-Six Views of Mount Fuji*, and British artist David Hockney, with his many interpretations of the swimming pools of California. All are part of a long list of renowned artists who have taken time to look at the same subject matter over and over again.

This is arguably a bit of an unfashionable idea: as a society, we're used to idolising the next big thing. We prioritise what's new. The notion of repeating or revisiting may suggest stagnation, or simply being left behind. With a typical knack for the provocative, Marcel Duchamp told one interviewer that the 'idea of repeating' was, for him, 'a form of masturbation'.[1] However, what's fashionable now is unlikely to remain so popular. Approach the idea of repeating yourself in the right mindset and you'll discover a way of working that helps you go beyond the surface and make your creative brain work that bit harder.

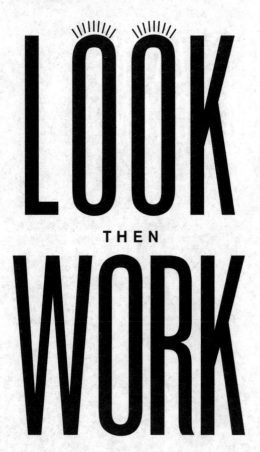

LOOK
THEN
WORK

It is beneficial to look closely. Quite often things are not quite as assumed. When Cézanne decided to start depicting Montagne Sainte-Victoire (from 1882), he was surprised to discover its shadow didn't appear exactly as he (and, in his words 'everyone else who fails to look') had thought.[2] The mountain offered ongoing revelations for him as he returned again and again, continuing his visits despite ailing health towards the end of his life. For Cézanne, nature was the greatest teacher. As he wrote to his fellow painter Émile Bernard in 1904, 'In order to make progress, there is only nature, and the eye is trained through contact with her. It becomes concentric through looking and working.'[3] Over 60 surviving examples show how the repeated process of simply 'looking and working' never produced the same result. It wasn't merely the viewpoint, or the conditions under which he painted that shifted. Cézanne used the mountain to study form and colour. Some depictions are detailed and precise, in others the form of the mountain is hazy and less discernable. While some are stripped down, others are densely layered with marks.

· ·

TAKE ANOTHER LOOK

As Cézanne shows us, there's always something new to see if you look closely enough. Pick something familiar in your immediate environment and subject it to scrutiny. Choose a patch of wall, your door, a kitchen chair or even your bedding. Hone in as much as you'd like. Take a pen, pencil or brush and try to capture its details and idiosyncrasies as faithfully as possible. Examine its texture, its markings, and how the light falls on it. Try doing the same at different times of the day and see what new details are revealed. What do you see differently each time you go back?

· ·

ONCE MORE,

WITH

FEELING

Also evidenced by the resulting work is Cézanne's connection with his subject matter. He wasn't drawn to Montagne Saint-Victoire simply for the challenge of depicting the mass of rock itself. The mountain ridge, near Cézanne's home in Aix-en-Provence, was part of the landscape of his childhood. His paintings in this series encompassed his memories, as well as what was in front of him. Rather than being a mechanical, technical exercise, each depiction of the scene drew on this connection. Find an object or motif that resonates with you and you'll discover something new each time you revisit it.

There's a parallel in the work of Yorkshire-born artist David Hockney. As Hockney flew into California for the first time in the 1960s, he noticed the number of swimming pools. Contrasting with his childhood in post-war Britain, these pools seemed to epitomise an alternative, modern way of living – the kind of life he had travelled to the United States to experience. They became a recurrent motif in his work of the mid-1960s.

What really attracted him, Hockney has said, was the technical challenge. 'It is a formal problem,' he explains, 'to represent water, to describe water, because it can be anything – it can be any colour, it's moveable, it has no set visual description.'[4] In some of Hockney's pools, the water resembles a camouflage pattern; in others, writhing lines of colour break up the surface. In *A Bigger Splash* (1967), the surface of the pool is a flat blue, painted with a roller. This skin is punctuated by the laboriously painted splash – according to Hockney, it took 'two weeks to paint this event that lasts for two seconds'.[5] Hockney's pools offer an interesting lesson. There is no single 'correct' answer to a problem. Indeed, the most creative solutions, such as that seen in *A Bigger Splash*, are more likely to come when you've spent significant time working through the problem.

BACK TO SQUARE ONE

This is a quick way to test your inventiveness under pressure. Draw yourself a grid of around 30 squares, each with space around it. These should all be the same size, around 2 × 2cm (1 × 1in), or slightly larger. Set a timer for three minutes and try to fill each of the squares in a different way. You could use different patterns and keep it abstract, or perhaps make the squares look like something else: for example, add a roof to make a house. Don't go back and edit – see how many squares you can fill in the time available. Notice how inventive you have to get as the time moves on.

MIX UP
YOUR
MEDIA

* → SOMETHING OLD, SOMETHING NEW (see p.76)

Even if the subject matter stays the same, the medium doesn't have to. Innovations are possible here, too. Just as Cézanne varied his depictions of Montagne Saint-Victoire using pencil, oil paints and watercolour, Hockney used his water theme to experiment with new materials. For *Paper Pools* (1978), he returned to the swimming pool motif but using coloured dyes and paper pulp. Water's representation 'couldn't be line,' he realised, 'it had to be mass, it had to be colour'.[6] A shift in medium may also shift the way that you think. ✱

This approach worked so well for Hockney, he has continued in his career by setting 'little problems' for himself, frequently devoting a significant chunk of time to exploring fully one motif or technique.[7] Think of *Woldgate Woods* (2010–11), a series of videos used to explore the changing seasons in his local Yorkshire landscape – these represent an intense period of observation and problem-solving, as well as an extension of the works on paper and canvas that Hockney produced after returning to his native county in the early 2000s. Repetition can be a way of escaping those much-feared creative ruts. It is a way of learning that can help you see your work in new ways – using the familiar to explore something new.

REPEAT REPEAT
REPEAT REPEAT
THE
ROUTINE

There's another form of repetition that underpins this work: not subject matter or technique, but that of routine. Hockney believes he has worked 'almost every day' for the last 60 years.[8] French artist Henri Matisse was similarly motivated, working from seven until noon each day, pausing for lunch, before picking up again and working until the early evening. The result? He claimed he was 'never bored'.[9] Catalan painter Joan Miró's rigid structure, meanwhile, involved work in the morning, a pause for lunch, cigarettes, exercise, a nap and correspondence, before returning to the studio for another five hours' work.[10] Taking away the mundane decisions of the everyday – when to eat, sleep, stop – not only organises time but liberates brain space, which you can put to much better use. ✻ Far from drudgery, it turns out that repetition – whether in work or routine – can be a way to find creative freedom.

✻ ⟶ MAKE SPACE (see p.38)

See this:

Paul Cézanne, *Montagne Sainte Victoire*, 1905–6

A watercolour depiction of Cézanne's beloved mountain, painted from a steeply terraced slope above the studio that Cézanne occupied from 1902 until his death in 1906.

David Hockney, *A Bigger Splash*, 1967

Perhaps the most abiding of Hockney's investigations into the Californian lifestyle.

Notes 1. Quoted in Karen Rosenberg, 'Paint It Once, Paint It Twice, Paint It Once Again', *New York Times*, 12 October 2007   2. Quoted in Richard Kendall (ed.), *Cézanne by Himself: Drawings, Paintings, Writings* (London: Macdonald Orbis, 1988), p.303   3. Quoted ibid., p.238   4. Quoted in Nikos Stangos (ed.), *Pictures by David Hockney* (London: Thames & Hudson, 1979), p.48   5. Quoted in Nikos Stangos (ed.), *David Hockney by David Hockney* (New York: Harry N. Abrams, 1976), p.124   6. Quoted in Peter Clothier, *David Hockney* (New York, London: Abbeville Press, 1995), p.43   7. Quoted in *David Hockney: Paintings, Prints and Drawings, 1960–1970* (London: Whitechapel Gallery, 1970), p.13   8. Quoted in John McDonald, 'Artist David Hockney: 80, Among the Most Experimental', https://www.afr.com/brand/afr-magazine/artist-david-hockney-80-among-the-most-experimental-20160606-gpckf7 <27 July 2016 (accessed 16 September 2018)>   9. Quoted in Mason Currey, *Daily Rituals: How Great Minds Make Time, Find Inspiration, and Get to Work* (London: Picador, 2013), p.4   10. Ibid., p.47

MAKE

SPACE

LUCIAN FREUD
AGNES MARTIN

You need space and time to create art. These might seem like simple requirements, but they don't usually present themselves without effort: it's all too easy for the artist to get distracted and discouraged and to lose track of priorities. Agnes Martin and Lucian Freud went to unusual extremes to achieve solitude and, although you may not want to replicate their working practices completely, they demonstrate the value of marking out and protecting your creative space.

A ROOM

OF YOUR OWN

A primary consideration for an artist is finding somewhere to be able to create. This may start small – artists such as Louise Bourgeois and Annette Messager have used their kitchen tables, out of necessity – but better, according to sculptor Lynda Benglis, echoing the famous words of Virginia Woolf, is to be able to 'find a room of your own'. Benglis says 'all artists need to heed that. It becomes your outer shell.'[1] Finding space can cost money, so consider a supposedly less desirable (and therefore less expensive) address. Removing yourself from the centre of a scene can also make you more productive. Lucian Freud deliberately sought out rooms in the unfashionable fringes of post-war London, while Agnes Martin chose to remove herself from New York, travelling for two years around the United States before arriving in a remote part of New Mexico in 1968. 'I must give independence a trial,' she wrote.[2]

Even if your working space consists of a single table, rather than a room of your own, it is valuable to create boundaries around it. Your work deserves the respect of being treated like work – rather than like the day's newspapers, accessible to all, easy to critique, and then to discard. Being able to create work without judgement fosters creative freedom; it encourages you to go with your gut, rather than what other people are telling you. Pablo Picasso, for example, didn't allow people to enter his Montparnasse studio in Paris without permission. Martin was equally insistent on keeping 'personal friends' out of her studio space,[3] insisting on 'cautious care' of the studio as a way of showing 'respect for the work'.[4]

Deliberately consider your studio space – how you want to set it up and what you want around you as you work. You could try drawing out your ideal situation and then seeing how much you can implement. Some artists, such as Francis Bacon, choose to surround themselves with their inspirations, while others prefer near-blankness. ✱ Marina Abramović describes how she really likes 'empty spaces, because my head is so full of things, and if I have these objects around me and on the wall, it's just too much to bear'.[5] Freud echoed Abramović's desire for emptiness. His studios were left deliberately bare, except for the marks where he had used the wall to wipe the excess off his paint tubes, and the bed and chairs on which his sitters would pose. Freud created work rooted in the studio, conveying the particular atmosphere generated between himself and his sitter. In his disquieting *Naked Portrait* (1972–3) (see

✱——→ COLLECT, RECOLLECT (see p.48)

page 104), for example, the almost animalistic form of the anonymous sitter is in counterpoint to Freud's inclusion of his artist's tools in the painting's foreground. Contrast this with the more domestic atmosphere of works by Alice Neel, such as *Kitty Pearson* (1973), in which the front room of Neel's New York apartment doubled as her studio. The space in which you create will influence your work.

SWITCH OFF TO BE

SWITCHED ON

Martin extolled the studio as a place for the artist to work without interruption. She believed that 'the artist works by awareness of his own state of mind. In order to do so she or he must have a studio, as a retreat and as a place to work. In the studio, the artist must have no interruptions from himself or anyone else. Interruptions are disasters.'[6] Paintings such as *Faraway Love* (1999), composed of bands of opaque, white acrylic gesso, overpainted with light blue Liquitex acrylic to create a light-reflecting finish, can be interpreted as capturing both her experience of landscape and the empty, egoless state of mind that she so carefully tried to maintain. 'Emptiness is what I want – zero when I'm painting and then eight hours later with no interruptions hopefully you've done some good painting', she said.[7]

Freud, too, was an expert in avoiding certain types of interruptions. He refused to own a cell phone or computer and gave very few people his home telephone number. Our lives are even more connected now than they were when Freud was working. Consider switching off your phone or computer, or at least moving them out of sight during the hours that you work – make it slightly harder to become distracted.

Making space is as much about finding time as it is the physical space in which to work. Forget – as best you can – the demands of other people and take control of your own time and how it is used. Martin wouldn't get out of bed until she knew what she wanted to paint that day, sometimes staying there until around 3pm. Freud would work in shifts: in the morning, and then in the night, working until the early hours. Describing his day he said, 'Basically, I'm a loner. I do as I please.'[8]

RETHINK
YOUR ROUTINE

Investigate the days of many successful creatives and you're likely to discover highly structured schedules, developed to hone productivity. Try one of these routines and see how it works for you. Robert Rauschenberg, for example, insisted on starting each day with a healthy breakfast, his vitamins and a double espresso, while Louise Bourgeois travelled to her studio every day at 10am, focusing on her sculpture first and last thing and drawing in the middle of the day. Emily Gosling's 2018 book *Great Minds Don't Think Alike* may help you to pick one such routine to follow for the day. Note when you feel most productive, and also least focused. Does the structure act as a support or a distraction? You could try out a couple of different patterns and then take your favourite elements to weave into your own day.

SET YOUR
SCENE

The self-chosen isolation of both Freud and Martin allowed them to focus on their own development. Freud's style – honed during the 1950s and '60s – stands in contrast to the outward-looking pop art style more commonly associated with the period. He chose to look inwards, rather than out to the commercialised world – to no further than the studio in front of him, in fact. Martin insisted that artists should consider themselves apart. 'The life of an artist is inspired, self-sufficient and independent (unrelated to society),' she said.[9] Martin used her isolation for self-reflection, untainted by the opinions of others, regularly destroying paintings that she determined to be disappointing.

Both artists were stubborn about their need to work. They saw the necessity of making art with a single-minded vision. 'To progress in life you must give up the things that you do not like,' advised Martin. 'You must find the things that you do like. The things that are acceptable to your mind.'[10]

PROCESS
THE PROCESS

What's stopping you from getting things done? Try planning your day by making a 'process map' to think through your working routine: chart out the plan for your day, drawing something to represent each activity and how long it might take you. Be as realistic as you can – adding in time to check emails, for example. Over a day, see how your plan works in reality. How much time is devoted to work? What don't you want to do? Can you drop any activities? Can you rearrange your day in a better way? Create a new, improved map and use it to guide your practice.

Although Martin discouraged 'personal friends' from visiting her studio, she didn't cut herself off entirely. She recommended allowing 'Friends of Art' into the studio – those 'who will not destroy the atmosphere but will bring encouragement and who are an absolute necessity in the field of art'.[11] Personal friends, she added, could be met in cafés. Like the ideas underpinning her work, however, this does mean being and staying in control. State your intention to work and stand by it – remove the people, places and things that might distract you from that aim. It's your responsibility to set the scene in which your creativity can flourish.

See this:

Lucian Freud, *Naked Portrait*, 1972–3

An unsettling glimpse into Freud's studio, with an unnamed sitter.

Agnes Martin, *Faraway Love*, 1999

A sense of the sublime captured through the stripping away of motif, colour and – according to the artist – distractions.

Notes 1. Quoted in James Cahill, *Ways of Being: Advice for Artists by Artists* (London: Laurence King, 2018), p.51 2. Agnes Martin. Letter to Leonore Tawney, 17 November 1967, quoted in Henry Martin, *Agnes Martin: Pioneer, Painter, Icon* (Tucson, AZ: Schaffner Press, 2018), p.187 3. Arne Glimcher, *Agnes Martin: Paintings, Writings, Remembrances* (London: Phaidon, 2012), p.30 of replica notebook 4. Ibid., p.33 of replica notebook 5. Quoted in Hans Ulrich Obrist, *Lives of the Artists, Lives of the Architects* (London: Allen Lane, 2015), p.249 6. Quoted in Sarah Lowndes, *Contemporary Artists Working Outside the City: Creative Retreat* (London: Routledge, 2018), unpaginated ebook 7. Quoted in Glimcher, p.100 8. Quoted in John Gruen, *The Artist Observed: 28 Interviews with Contemporary Artists* (Chicago, IL: A Cappella Books, 1991), p.322 9. Quoted in Glimcher, p.123 10. Quoted in Barbara Haskell, *Agnes Martin* (New York: Whitney Museum of American Art, 1992), p.12 11. Glimcher, p.30 of replica notebook

COLLECT

RE-

COLLECT

FRANCIS BACON
ANTHEA HAMILTON
ANNETTE MESSAGER

★ —→ CURIOUSER & CURIOUSER (see p.18)

Feed your creativity to keep it alive. A part of creating is delving deeper into what's around you. ★ 'I look at everything,' said Francis Bacon, and accounts of his workspace bear this out: his studio was piled high with photographs of work by artists such as Goya, Rembrandt and Picasso, alongside pornography, books on radiography and photographic sources such as the pictures of Eadweard Muybridge.[1] All of these references fed into Bacon's work.

The artist and the collector are closely linked. The word 'studio' comes from the Latin *studium*, meaning pursuit or zeal, as well as study, and there are countless examples of artists zealously collecting, from Claude Monet and his Japanese prints to Martin Parr's 'boring postcards', to Tacita Dean's four-leaved clovers. Whatever you are interested in, seek it out; it will probably tell you something about yourself and your work. American artist Joan Jonas has collected masks and artefacts from around the world and used them regularly in her performances. ✱ Jonas is interested in masks because they not only hide her face, but also suggest different identities to explore: 'If you put a mask on you can enter a different world', she has said.[2] Meanwhile, Andy Warhol's personal collection encompassed everything from mid-century Russel Wright tableware and cookie jars to American Indian artefacts and priceless works of art. In his own work, Warhol embraced and combined 'high' and 'low' culture.

While you may not want to go to the extremes of Bacon or Warhol (whose collection made up 10,000 lots in a ten-day auction following his death[3]), it's worth building a modest hoard of things that inspire and intrigue to which you can return when you need a prompt. Think of it as a store cupboard, stocked for leaner periods. An artist's collection is often the key to their practice. Let yours motivate, inspire, influence and change your work. Let it become an obsession.

If storage space is at a premium, you can always keep your collection in a different or more condensed form. Bacon devoted his whole studio to what interested him, but you just need to figure out a way of creating a collection that's both easy to update and, like Bacon's, easy to access. Carry a sketchbook with you at all times – David Hockney has special pockets sewn into his suits and coats so that he always has a sketchbook, or his iPad, to hand. Use it to curate a visual library of experiences and

✱
|
KEEP ON MOVING (see p.66)

things that interest you. Pop art pioneer Eduardo Paolozzi filled scrap-books with collected imagery that informed works such as the collage series *Meet the People* (1948). Don't worry about giving the material in your sketch- or scrapbooks an order – the collision of different materials will help spark ideas.

You can also collect digitally, if that's your preference. Contemporary artist Christian Marclay uses his camera like a sketchbook, collecting 'visual references, interesting coincidences, things I find curious or funny, or that I might be able to use later on in my work. It could be an object, a poster, a flower, or anything that captures my attention or triggers an idea.'[4] He describes it as a 'magnifying glass', getting him to pay close attention to what's around him.[5]

EVERYTHING IS A

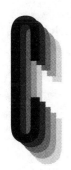

Learning by copying past masters has been part of art education for centuries. Rather than simply imitating an artist or work of art in terms of subject matter, you can analyse the elements that are most valuable to you and the emotions they evoke. Take, for example, Diego Velázquez's 1650 portrait of Pope Innocent X. Contemplating it almost exactly three centuries later, Bacon found that it triggered 'all sorts of feelings' for him –

so much so that he worked on paintings relating to its imagery for over 20 years.[6] It became part of his visual reference library, interrogated both for how it looked and how it made him feel. Demand the same of your own visual influences and, if they're not giving you satisfactory answers, try this process.

COPY

» Tear out pictures from a newspaper or magazine. Which images resonate with you? Why?

» Look closer. Which specific elements of the images intrigue you? Why?

» Copy one of these elements, using your own method.

» Repeat, changing just one thing about your method. For example, copy onto newsprint rather than plain paper, or change your medium.

» Repeat again and again, changing one more thing each time.

» Incorporate one or more of your copies into something that you are making.

» Try this exercise regularly to see what new possibilities it inspires.

When Bacon saw a film still of the screaming woman in Sergei Eisenstein's silent film *Battleship Potemkin* (1925), he declared it the best depiction of a cry he'd seen, and incorporated aspects into his own work. The mouth and glasses can be identified in *Study for a Portrait* (1952) (see page 105), for example. Bacon absorbed everything and his influences reappeared, in his own words, 'ground up very fine' within his work.[7] What Bacon called his 'imagination material' drew widely and freely from a range of sources.[8] Anything can be potential material.

THE REORDER OF THINGS

If Bacon used his collection as a source, Annette Messager uses hers in the substance of her work. She's known for adopting different characters and one of the earliest was 'Annette Messager *collectionneuse*'. Compared to the artist in her studio, the *collectionneuse* worked in her bedroom. In this role as collector, she made 56 albums over the period 1971–4. The albums echoed the forms of scrapbooks or diaries, the kinds of items made in homes over many years. Messager's process was to 'inspect, collect, order, sort, and reduce everything'.[9] She put together albums on different themes, often using material from lifestyle magazines. *Children with Their Eyes Scratched Out No 3* (1971–2) is made up of photographs of children whose eyes have been obliterated by Messager's scrawl, and *Voluntary Tortures* (1972) is a compilation of images showing women undergoing painful beauty treatments. The artist gives a new context to the images that we see every day. Messager wrote in 1973, 'I seek to possess and appropriate for myself life and its events.'[10] She shows how collecting gives you not only control, but also power.

Messager describes how she likes 'bric-a-brac, tinkering around, making different genres collide…I like being able to refer to Edward Lear and James Ensor without establishing a hierarchy, putting on the same plane William Blake and Walt Disney, comedy and tragedy, the sublime and the tacky.'[11] Like Bacon and Warhol, Messager combines inspiration from different cultural registers and isn't afraid to get her hands dirty in the process. Follow her creative cue and have fun 'tinkering around'.

· ·

FOLLOW YOUR OWN ORDERS

Messager explores links between materials, images and words. Inspired by her example, imagine that you are compiling your own illustrated dictionary. Collect a stack of colour magazines: art magazines, fashion magazines, gossip magazines – the more varied the better. Open a dictionary at random and pick a word that appeals. Combine images and text from the magazines to build up a visual representation of that word according to your personal associations. For example, 'bird' might imply not only the animal, but also its characteristics, the use of the word as slang and even your specific memories. Let your associations range as widely as possible. Make as many pages of your dictionary as you'd like, noticing any themes that recur.

· ·

TAKE IT
ELSEWHERE

When asked what her favourite book was, Messager replied that it would be a dictionary. 'I can look at a dictionary for hours and in this way I can dream,' she said. 'The words in it lead on to other words and you can get lost in them.'[12] Bacon described the process of getting from piles of ephemera to some of the greatest works of the 20th century as 'a chain of ideas created by various images that I look at'.[13] There's a similar chain at work in the three-dimensional collages of Anthea Hamilton. She makes no effort to disguise her source material, but leaves the role of interpretation to the viewer. The inspiration for *The Squash* (Tate Britain Commission 2018), in which a performer, clad in a vegetable-inspired costume, inhabits a specially constructed, white-tiled environment, came from a photograph of a man dressed in a vegetable suit that she found in a book about improvisational theatre and art from the 1960s and '70s. In her 2016 *Project for Door (After Gaetano Pesce),* an oversized pair of splayed buttocks is a hypothetical 1970s proposal by architect Pesce brought to life.

Hamilton has a collector's mindset, looking for links among disparate sources: 'The skill in my work is more about play,' she says, 'being deft in spotting visual associations of material rather than manipulating them through craft.'[14] Inspiration can be found anywhere: she unearths raw material on the high street, as well as in flea markets. The collected items become three-dimensional collages, which she then combines to tell her story.

Hamilton's aim is to bring about a 'physical knowledge of images', creating a bodily response to, as well as a visual perception of, what we see.[15] Her work is humorous but there are always deeper levels to discover, with each piece blending popular culture, art history and Hamilton's personal life, although you wouldn't necessarily recognise the biographical elements on first viewing. The viewer can delve as deep as they wish, and there is no definitive interpretation. As Hamilton puts it: 'I push for ambiguity.'[16] Follow her example and make your collected images and objects work harder.

WHERE CAN YOU TAKE IT?

1. Head to the shops and pick up a handful of inexpensive objects. Look closely at each object. Of what do they remind you?

2. Work out how each object instinctively makes you feel. Perhaps it makes you smile? Perhaps it makes you want to touch it?

3. Carry out additional research on each object. You might investigate its material, function or history. What new things can you discover about the objects?

4. Imagine you have to convey the idea of the object and what it stands for to someone else, without simply replicating its appearance. What would you focus on: its texture, its function, something from its history or something else entirely?

Of course, a collection is very rarely declared complete – it can always be, in Messager's words, 'more and more beautiful, bigger and bigger, always incomplete'.[17] There's always more to look at, to engage with, to order. You, the collector, are in charge – what do you want to do?

See this:

Francis Bacon, *Study for a Portrait*, 1952

The cry from Eisenstein's *Battleship Potemkin*, as filtered by the eye of Bacon.

Annette Messager, *The Pikes*, 1992–3

A boundary-blurring installation, where high art meets low, and art meets craft to evoke a revolutionary spirit.

Eduardo Paolozzi, *Meet the People*, 1948

Paolozzi was a compulsive scrapbooker; this collage uses imagery taken from American magazines.

Notes 1. Quoted in Kitty Hauser, *This is Bacon* (London: Laurence King, 2014), p.6
2. Quoted in Susan Morgan, *Joan Jonas: I Want to Live in the Country (and Other Romances)*
(London: Afterall Books. 2006), p.81 3. Lydia Yee. *Magnificent Obsessions: the Artist as
Collector* (London: Prestel, 2015), p.14 4. Quoted in Jean-Pierre Criqui. *On&By Christian
Marclay* (London: Whitechapel Gallery, 2015), p.66 5. Quoted ibid. 6. David Sylvester, *The
Brutality of Fact: Interviews with Francis Bacon* (London: Thames & Hudson, 1987). p.24
7. Quoted in Hauser, p.6 8. Quoted in Francis Giacobetti. 'Francis Bacon: The Last Interview',
https://www.independent.co.uk/arts-entertainment/art/features/francis-bacon-the-last-
interview-8368727.html <14 June 2003 (accessed 17 September 2018)> 9. Quoted in
Sheryl Conkelton and Carol S. Eliel, *Annette Messager* (London; Thames & Hudson: New
York: Museum of Modern Art, 1995), p.59 10. Quoted ibid. 11. Quoted ibid., p.43 12.
Quoted in Charles Arsène-Henry. Shumon Basar and Karen Marta (eds), *Hans Ulrich Obrist
Interviews: Volume 2* (Milan: Charta, 2010), p.506 13. Quoted in Giacobetti 14. Quoted
in 'Anthea Hamilton Exhibited at the Saatchi Gallery'. https://www.saatchigallery.com/artists/
anthea_hamilton.htm <accessed 19 September 2018> 15. Quoted in Laura Smith and
Linsey Young, *Turner Prize 2016* (London: Tate Publishing, 2016), p.21 16. Quoted in Harriet
Baker, 'Interview with Turner Prize Nominee Anthea Hamilton'. https://www.ft.com/content/
bd4d502e-a4df-11e6-8898-79a99e2a4de6, <11 November 2016 (accessed 19 September
2018)> 17. Quoted in 'Annette Messager by Bernard Marcade'. *BOMB 26*, Winter. 1989,
pp.28–33

MAKE IT UP AS YOU GO ALONG

ALBERTO GIACOMETTI
REBECCA WARREN

It is easy to imagine that really great pieces of art are always the results of meticulous planning – that experts plan, and only amateurs try to think on their feet. But if art were only about following a set of instructions to arrive at a predetermined result, there would be no creative process. Rather than looking forward, try to live in the moment. Embrace the opportunities available to you only in that second and trust in your own intuition.

Practise thinking on your feet. Try abstract painter Agnes Martin's way of working: 'by inspiration' rather than 'by intellect'; improvise, don't analyse.[1] When you're working, it's time to switch off the buzz of your brain and the worries of the day and, instead, tune into all of your five senses, listening to what they are telling you. Or, as British sculptor Rebecca Warren puts it, 'you have to make it all from a good unconscious place, not your ego'.[2] It is not the time to criticise your work (you can do that later), but to create. The more you improvise, the more flexible you'll become, and the more your creativity will increase. You may end up somewhere completely different to where you expected – but isn't that the whole point?

Begin with purpose but without an exact plan. ✱ Step into the unknown. Swiss artist Alberto Giacometti expressed the improvisational nature of this step when he said, 'I want something, but I won't know what it is until I succeed in doing it.'[3] With his sculptures and paintings, he was attempting to capture images he had in his own head, rather than simply copying reality. He tried to work 'without stopping to ask myself what [these images] might mean'.[4] Don't overthink. You don't need to be entirely sure what you're doing – in fact, it's probably better if you don't.

This is not to say you need to rush – speeding along to outrun your critical brain. Giacometti used the idea of a blind man, feeling his way into the night, as a metaphor for creativity.[5] Progress steadily, thoughtfully, with intuition. The quickest solutions are unlikely to be the most interesting ones. To echo the best advice Warren says she was ever given: 'Stay with it, don't force it.'[6]

Warren's works hover in a state between the clay from which they were made and the objects and subjects she wants to represent. She describes her process: 'You're heading in some kind of direction, mostly blindly, but

✱ —— JUST DO IT (see p.8)

with eyes wide open, so that your whole attention is focused on what the work is trying to be. You're following it around and you're hopeful. You don't push it, but you also try not to lag behind.'[7] Gradually, a form develops: 'At some point it becomes clear what the thing wants to be.'[8] In a work such as *Versailles* (2006) (see pages 106–7), roughly fashioned forms of a breast, flowers and a hand seem to emerge from the mass of clay, in a delicate balance of submergence and emergence. For Warren, knowing where that balance is to be found, and when she needs to stop working, is part of the challenge.

EYES WIDE SHUT

Start trusting your intuition. Find an object to draw. Study it, touch it, ask yourself what it reminds you of. Now close your eyes and try to sketch the object on a piece of paper. Do this reasonably quickly to capture your impressions. Open your eyes, and try the exercise again with the object in front of you. Compare the two resulting drawings.

ALL PART OF THE

PROCESS

Giacometti's sculptures were often made over long periods, with time devoted to them in intensive bursts. He worked and reworked them many times over. Even if he made something he was satisfied with, he sometimes remade it, 'to see if it'll succeed as well the second time'.[9] Giacometti shows us how the process of making – its sense of possibility – can be more invigorating than the final result. Being an 'artist' is not only about the artwork you end up with but also the process you go through.

Like those of a jazz improviser, Giacometti's methods challenge the notion that there is one definite endpoint that an artist is striving towards. *Woman of Venice IX* (1956) is one of ten figures Giacometti made for the Venice Biennale, in a process observed by the critic David Sylvester. Giacometti created a single standing figure using his usual method of building up clay over a wire armature. When he liked what he'd done, he would have a plaster cast taken, before continuing to work on the sculpture. From this array of casts in various states of 'finish', Giacometti selected and made the ten bronzes for the Biennale. As Sylvester described: 'The last of the states was no more definitive than its predecessors.'[10]

Have the courage to see where your work can take you and it may have surprising results. For Warren, her works are not over-determinedly planned so much as they are 'exposures of my intimate relations to art and the world'.[11] Giacometti would sometimes 'recognise images, impressions and experiences – transformed and displaced – which have moved me very deeply, often without me being aware of it'.[12] Unconsciously, the phases of the work become a record of you as an artist at that particular moment in time. Like Giacometti's records of his bronzes in various states of 'finish', you might photograph the piece you are working on every hour, or perhaps at the end of each working day – this record of your progress might provide real insight into the routes towards the finished work and its possible variants.

FIND YOUR PURPOSE

Have a purpose, not a plan. Knowing what you want your work to achieve, rather than how you plan to achieve it, will guide you. Write your own artist's manifesto. In a manifesto, you should outline what you stand for: your core beliefs, how you intend for your work to reflect these and the kind of world to which you wish your work to contribute. Use the first person to reinforce your statements – 'I believe', 'I intend' – and edit to make your statements as concise and memorable as possible. Write out your manifesto and embellish it with symbols that reinforce your statement. Display this prominently as a reminder of what you're trying to achieve to help guide you through times of uncertainty.

FAIL WELL

When you work in an improvisational way, you don't know what will happen. As Warren notes, 'there is no definitive way of predicting a successful outcome'.[13] Some things just aren't going to work in the way you would want them to. There will be occasions when 'you have totally messed something up, only to realize that it was right in the first place'.[14] Not giving up is another valuable part of the process.

All this goes back to the idea of 'being' creative. Trying new things and seeing where they lead might take you to dazzling new heights or, unfortunately, sometimes the corresponding depths, but, in the words of Vincent van Gogh, 'If one wants to be active, one mustn't be afraid to do something wrong sometimes, not afraid to lapse into some mistakes. To be good – many people think that they'll achieve it by doing no harm – and that's a lie...That leads to stagnation, to mediocrity.'[15] Creativity doesn't come from trying to stay still.

Neither does creativity hinge on the mistakes themselves – an inevitable consequence of being brave and trying new things – but the artistic expertise you gain from making them. 'Whether it fails or whether it comes off in the end becomes secondary,' said Giacometti, 'I advance in any case. Whether I advance by failing or whether I advance by gaining a little, I'll always have gained for myself.'[16] Don't get hung up on your failures. Note them and then move on. There's always something new to learn.

See this:

Alberto Giacometti, *Woman of Venice IX*, 1956

One of Giacometti's ten 'finished' sculptures for the Venice Biennale.

Rebecca Warren, *Versailles*, 2006

Consider why Warren thought of this work as finished at this exact point in her process. What would have happened if she'd continued working on it?

Notes 1. Quoted in Madeleine Grynsztejn, *The Art of Richard Tuttle* (San Francisco, CA: San Francisco Museum of Modern Art, 2005), p.25   2. Quoted in Rebecca Warren and Laura Smith, 'Interview: Rebecca Warren – "From the mess of experience"', https://www.tate.org.uk/tate-etc/issue-41-autumn-2017/rebecca-warren-interview-from-the-mess-of-experience <6 September 2017 (accessed 19 September 2018)>   3. 'The Champ of the Prize Winners', *Life*, 29 May 1964, p.95   4. Quoted in Simon Wilson, *Surrealist Painting* (London: Phaidon Press, 1994), p.38   5. James Cahill, *Ways of Being: Advice for Artists by Artists* (London: Laurence King, 2018), p.36   6. Fergal Stapleton, quoted by Rebecca Warren in Laura Barnett, 'Portrait of the Artist: Rebecca Warren, Sculptor', https://www.theguardian.com/artanddesign/2009/apr/07/sculptor-rebecca-warren <7 April 2009 (accessed 20 September 2018)>   7. Quoted in Kelly Baum, Andrea Bayer and Sheena Wagstaff, *Unfinished: Thoughts Left Visible* (New York: Metropolitan Museum of Art, 2016), p.256   8. Quoted ibid. 9. Quoted in David Sylvester, *Looking at Giacometti* (London: Chatto & Windus, 1994), p.134 10. Ibid.   11. Quoted in Warren and Smith   12. Alberto Giacometti, 'Je ne puis parler qu'indirectement de mes sculptures', *Minotaure*, Nos 3–4, December 1933, p.46   13. Quoted in Baum, Bayer and Wagstaff, p.258   14. Quoted ibid.   15. Vincent van Gogh to Theo van Gogh, 2 October 1884, quoted in Patrick Grant, *Reading Vincent van Gogh: A Thematic Guide to the Letters* (Edmonton, Alberta: AU Press, 2016), p.86   16. Quoted in Sylvester, p.136

KEEP ON MOVING

ROBERT FRANK
PAUL GAUGUIN
JOAN JONAS

When you're feeling stuck, move. From the smallest kind of move – getting up and walking around – to the largest, such as changing cities, even countries, moving is a way of getting a new viewpoint. When you move, you gain something essential for an artist: a new perspective.

Small movements can make for great leaps forward. Sick of staring at the walls around your desk? Move your desk. Creative block? Perhaps that's symptomatic of being physically stuck in one position – so move your body. Incorporate excuses to move into your day. Something as simple as going to put the kettle on can break the inertia – the author Roddy Doyle suggests that a writer keep her or his thesaurus in the shed. If you have a specific problem, try acting it out, letting the movement of your body reflect what you are trying to do on paper or canvas.

MOVE
YOUR
MIND

Echo performance artist Joan Jonas, who describes choreography as 'drawing in space'.[1] For her, the smallest, simplest moves can be a prompt to creativity. Jonas often incorporates props into her work – cues to start moving the body in a different way. Think about ways to use your body to jolt it out of its usual routine.

Moving the body moves the mind. The benefits of something as simple as going for a walk have long been noted. The philosopher Friedrich Nietzsche wrote: 'All truly great thoughts are conceived by walking.'[2] Marina Abramović says that she's often found solutions to problems when doing 'something completely different' – 'hiking, walking or swimming'.[3] The advantages of exercise for creativity are proven, though the reasons for this are less well understood. Exercise is thought to provide space in which the mind can wander, with effects that linger even after the activity has finished. While artists don't always have a reputation for good health, there are many who have harnessed the benefits of movement: American artist Georgia O'Keeffe, for example, took a 30-minute walk first thing on most days, while Spanish painter Joan Miró ensured exercise was always part of his routine, enjoying everything from boxing to gymnastics.

LEARN THE ART OF
TRAVEL

Move farther. Travel has inspired artists for centuries – a boost to creativity with many different benefits.

A new setting can provide new subject matter for your art. Experience the art and culture of a place directly, rather than relying on reproductions. Follow the example of Flemish artist Peter Paul Rubens, who spent several years travelling in Italy at the start of the 17th century, or English landscape and portrait painter Joseph Wright of Derby, who undertook his own pilgrimage the following century with a similar aim of understanding and learning from the art of antiquity.

Looking at different artistic traditions broadens your aesthetic vision and challenges preconceived ideas of how things should look and why. The objects that Joan Jonas collects on her travels play an essential role in her work, allowing her to continually revise and enrich both her worldview and her aesthetic. Paper kites found by Jonas in a small village in Vietnam were used in the installation *Stream or River, Flight or Pattern* (2016–17). The masks she collects offer prompts for movement, as they hint at old legends and suggest new stories. Jonas also films as she travels. The footage used in *Stream or River, Flight or Pattern* comes from Italy, Singapore, Spain and India, with Jonas turning her camera in each place to record the things that interest her – 'birds, trees, rituals' – and allowing her experiences to create new meanings.[4] Jonas stores up the memories from these travels – in the form of footage and the objects that she encounters – like a collection. ★ It means that, even when shut away in her studio, she can recapture an experience. 'In order to stay in my studio all the time,' Jonas says, 'I need to go out and bring things back from my travels.'[5] The benefits of travel can far outlast the actual journey.

Travel can also suggest different modes of thinking. Jonas's work is underpinned by the idea of ritual, an interest that has emerged through

★ | ↓

COLLECT, RECOLLECT (see p.48)

her travels. In the late 1960s, when she started making her first works, she spent a few months in a small village in Crete, where she witnessed 'rituals of everyday life'.[6] She was also exposed to other forms of ritual: in the late 1960s in the southwest of the United States, where she saw the Snake Dance of the Hopi Native American people, and in 1970 in Japan, where she discovered Noh theatre. In the deliberate movements of Noh and its separation of sound and text from action she saw an alternative to the prevailing minimalism of the period. She worked to 'translate [these elements] into my own language',[7] combining ideas, moods and, in the case of Noh theatre specifically, the use of the mask, which has become a common motif in her work.

DRAWING IN THE SAND

Joan Jonas's work frequently references other rituals. Her work *Lines in the Sand* (2002) echoes a New Guinea death ritual, in which the completion of a line in the sand assures the passage to the next world after death.[8] Many of Jonas's works make a performance out of drawing, emphasising the process rather than the result. Using sand as your canvas is not only a calming way to make art, it's also a way to be creative without getting too hung up on its final appearance. Find a sandy beach, or use other natural materials such as mud or dry soil. Use a rake or a stick to draw large, bold marks in the material. Mix up the kind of patterns you make: from sweeping arcs to short staccato strokes. Your own movements – your footprints – will also become part of the work. Have fun experimenting knowing that the sea (or the rain) will soon wash your artwork away.

When Paul Gauguin left France, first for Martinique in 1887, then Tahiti in 1891, he also hoped to find something else. He wanted a new kind of art – one endowed with a spirituality that he believed was lacking in the Western world. He had ambitions to break from impressionism and wanted to escape the pressures and insularity of Paris and forge a career on different terms – to literally gain some distance from his rivals. He saw his move to Tahiti as a way to escape the everyday, to create a new way of living. Like many in the period, he wanted to turn his back on the apparent horrors of industrialisation and find a pure, untouched paradise. Gauguin indulged in the fantasy of travel in works such as *Faa Iheihe* (1898) (see pages 108–9), which depicts such a place, where humans can live harmoniously with nature. This painting pulsates with bold, intense colours and the suggestion of a spirituality that lies just beyond our comprehension. It is a seductive vision, but one that's more Gauguin's fantasy than reality. In his unsatisfactory search for the 'wild and the primitive', the artist moved from Brittany to Martinique to Tahiti and then, finally, to the island of Hiva Oa.[9]

GO ON A MICROADVENTURE

You needn't go to the other side of the world. Some of travel's perspective-shifting benefits can be harnessed with a 'microadventure': a term devised by author Alastair Humphreys to describe an easily achievable expedition that happens close to home. Give these ideas a go:

» Go on a night-time hike.

» Camp in your back garden.

» Stay on a train until the last stop.

» Take a walk with each turn determined by the toss of a coin.

» Pick a random spot on a map of your local area and travel there.

EXPLORE THE
UNKNOWN

Gauguin travelled with a fixed idea of what he was looking for, but it can also be advantageous to be open to what you might find. ✱ Putting yourself somewhere unfamiliar can help you see the world in a new way, as demonstrated by the work of photographer Robert Frank. Swiss born, he emigrated to the United States in 1946 and travelled frequently, making sequences of work in Peru, Cuba, Panama, Brazil, Bolivia, England and Wales. However, it was the outsider perspective he brought to work shot closer to his (new) home that really made his name. He spent nine months between 1955 and 1956 criss-crossing the United States, taking the photographs that would be published as *The Americans* (first published in France in 1959, the book was released in the US in 1960). Frank visited more than 30 states, covering over 16,000 kilometres (nearly 10,000 miles). He purposefully picked out motifs that might be unremarkable to native eyes but to him said something about America: cars, cowboys, flags, jukeboxes. As he travelled, he experienced a different side of the country, especially in the South. His images highlight class and race tensions – for example, the photograph of the segregated streetcar in New Orleans that was used on the cover of the first US edition of the book – and were at odds with the optimistic way in which America presented itself in the

✱ ⟶ CURIOUSER & CURIOUSER (see p.18)

period. Through his travels, he could observe this reality for himself and capture what he saw with his own fresh perspective.

Moving is a simple way to wake up and revitalise the mind. Whether you're moving across a room or halfway around the world, it can help you not only see different things, but see things differently. And being able to see things differently is at the core of being able to think creatively.

See this:

Robert Frank, contact sheets from *The Americans*, 1955–6, printed 1970s

Frank reviewed more than 27,000 frames for his book project, a very small proportion of which are shown here.

Paul Gauguin, *Faa Iheihe*, 1898

Painted by Gauguin in Tahiti and depicting the island as a kind of earthly paradise.

Joan Jonas, *The Juniper Tree*, 1976, reconstructed 1994

The artist's first installation piece: a reinterpretation of a Brothers Grimm fairy tale – her props included a Japanese kimono.

Notes 1. Quoted in M. K. Palomar, 'Joan Jonas: "I Often Went to Magic Shows as a Child, and the Idea of Magic and Sleight of Hand Had a Big Effect on Me"', https://www.studiointernational.com/index.php/joan-jonas-interview-tate-modern <2 May 2018 (accessed 19 September 2018)> 2. Quoted in Marily Oppezzo and Daniel L. Schwartz, 'Give Your Ideas Some Legs: The Positive Effect of Walking on Creative Thinking', *Journal of Experimental Psychology: Learning, Memory, and Cognition*, Vol.40, No.4, pp.1142–52 3. Quoted in Thomas Boutoux (ed.), *Hans Ulrich Obrist Interviews: Volume 1* (Milan: Charta, 2003), pp.30–1 4. Quoted in 'Joan Jonas: "I Am Curious About Life"', https://www.tate.org.uk/art/artists/joan-jonas-7726/joan-jonas-i-am-curious-about-life <16 March 2018 (accessed 19 September 2018)> 5. Quoted in Charles Arsène-Henry, Shumon Basar and Karen Marta (eds), *Hans Ulrich Obrist Interviews: Volume 2* (Milan: Charta, 2010), p.388 6. Quoted ibid. 7. Quoted ibid. 8. Jane Philbrick, '(Re)viewing "Lines in the Sand" and Other Key Works of Joan Jonas', *A Journal of Performance and Art*, Vol. 26, No. 3 (September 2004), pp. 17–29 9. Quoted in Belinda Thompson (ed.), *Gauguin: Maker of Myth* (London: Tate Publishing, 2010), p.111

SOMETHING OLD, SOMETHING NEW

HELENA ALMEIDA
HENRI MATISSE
GRAYSON PERRY

Don't keep doing the same old thing trying to get new results. Kickstart your creativity by exploring alternative techniques and mediums. Louise Bourgeois reminds us: 'Material is only material. It is there to serve you and give you the best it can. If you are not satisfied, if you want more, you go to another material.'[1] Play. Inspiration may strike as you engage with a traditional craft, or might perhaps be triggered by tinkering with the photo-editing software on your phone. Try experimenting to find something that works for you and what you want to say. Not all experiments are successful, but they can lead you onto a new path, or help you reconsider past ones. Have fun giving new (old) things a try.

DON'T FEAR THE

FUTURE

★ ⟶ REPEAT, REPEAT, REPEAT (see p.28)

Historically, the introduction of new technology, such as video or photography, has often been treated with suspicion – how could they be art? At an early meeting of the Photographic Society of London in 1853, for example, one member described the technique as 'too literal' and unable to 'elevate the imagination'.[2] New innovations, however, can be an opportunity rather than a threat. 'Technology has always contributed to art,' argues David Hockney. 'The brush itself is a piece of technology, isn't it?'[3] Hockney has enthusiastically embraced new ideas throughout his career, experimenting with faxes, photocopiers and iPads in his attempts to solve specific problems. ★ He considers these experiments in using or repurposing modern devices as embodying the 'spirit of research', and it is this process of discovery that most interests him: 'I am not so much interested in the mere objects I'm creating as in where they're taking me.'[4] It's always worth trying something out – discovering for yourself what it can and can't do, or perhaps what it could do in the future.

FASHION

THE

UNFASH-IONABLE

As well as exploring new technology, there is sometimes value in revisiting techniques that have been neglected by the art world. British artist Grayson Perry famously catapulted the 'craft' of pottery into high art. Its unfashionable reputation was exactly why it appealed – the art world's avoidance (and the general public's acceptance) of the craft was a fault line that he could explore. 'I can be as outrageous as I like here because the vice squad is never going to raid a pottery exhibition', he said.[5] Works such as *Aspects of Myself* (2001) are made using traditional methods – this pot's shape was built up in clay using a coiling method, with layers of coloured slip, lustre glaze and ceramic transfers applied to the work which required multiple firings. Less traditional is the subject matter. The pot is decorated with images ranging from the everyday, like a man on a motorbike, to the more unsettling, such as a gagged and bound woman. As the title suggests, the work explores aspects of the artist's life and personality, from his childhood to his interest in sadomasochism. Perry has described such pieces as 'stealth bombs', bringing provocative imagery and, in other works, issues such as child abuse into the gallery, confounding the expectations of the viewer.[6]

Perry's art is very different to Hockney's, but they share the same spirit of exploration: trying out different techniques and mediums, and seeing where they lead. Perry established his reputation with pottery but has also employed tapestry, embroidery, printmaking and architecture to make his art; he even created a cast-iron coffin ship for his 2011 British Museum exhibition 'The Tomb of the Unknown Craftsman'. Perry himself notes that it took him 10 to 15 years from his first pottery lesson as an adult and almost 30 years from his very first lesson in primary school to fully realise what he could do with the medium. 'Even now it's up for grabs,' he says. 'I enjoy pottery but it's not as if I was born to do it. In ten years' time I could make vases as a sideline if something else came along that I was

passionate about.'[7] Technology is changing things
traditional crafts. Perry, for example, believes that
save craftsmanship because it 'separates creative pro
of production'.[8] Of the infinite possibilities that are
comments: 'A computer is more blank than any blank ca

Trying something new (or reviving something neglected) isn't just about change for change's sake. It can trigger fresh ways of thinking and working. As Perry says, 'It's also a great joy to learn a technique, because as soon as you learn it, you start thinking in it. When I learn a new technique my imaginative possibilities have expanded.'[10] Give your brain something new to chew over and it can reinvigorate what you already know: making connections between two seemingly unrelated things often results in great invention.

MAKE THE CONNECTION

One creative hack is to 'force' connections between things. Try picking random words out of a dictionary, for example, and then apply them to the problem you want to solve. You can also use a more visual approach. Find some strips of scrap paper and write on them the names of different objects. Make the selection as far-ranging as possible: doll, lamp, fork, wheelbarrow. Put the strips into a bowl and then pull out two at random. Your challenge is to combine them in a drawing. For example, the fork could be shown attached to the wheel of the wheelbarrow and used to aerate soil. See how many of these hybrids you can invent.

BASICS

Artistic innovation doesn't necessarily involve adopting a radically new approach – it can often come out of techniques that you are already familiar with, when seen in a new light. After an operation late in life left him greatly weakened, French artist Henri Matisse found a new way of working. He created gouache *découpées*, or 'cut-outs', made by cutting or tearing shapes from paper painted with gouache. He had previously used pieces of paper to work out arrangements within his paintings – now he realised the technique had potential in its own right, and that the simple tools of paper and scissors could be used more inventively. Matisse described it as 'a simplification': 'Instead of drawing the outline and putting the colour inside it – the one modifying the other – I draw straight into the colour.'[11] He sometimes cut directly into paper to make the shapes rather than tracing a shape first – a process described by Jacqueline Duhême, one of his studio assistants, as 'like making a sculpture'.[12] *The Snail* (1953) (see page 112) was made by Matisse asking his assistants to pin pieces of roughly torn paper onto a white background, then adjusting the papers' positions until the composition met with his approval. The work presents an abstracted version of a snail, the artist playing as much with colour as shape: the final arrangement pairs complementary colours such as orange and blue in close proximity. The number of pinpricks that can be seen in some of the component cut-outs illustrate just how frequently these pieces were moved to meet Matisse's exacting standards.

There are always new ways to invent – sometimes you just need to look sideways to find them. Helena Almeida described herself as a painter, but, in her interrogation of what a painting is, she used photography, drawing and her own body to test the medium's limits. She wanted to create 'a path connecting several media'.[13] Works such as *Drawing (with Pigment)* (1995–9) are preparation for her photography and video works, outlining ideas for physical actions. In what she calls 'Inhabited Canvases', her actions disturb our conception of each medium's limits: a splash of blue paint interrupts a photographic image, or she is photographed stepping around and across a canvas frame.

ON THE OTHER HAND

A very simple way to start thinking about using basic tools differently is to try to draw with your non-dominant hand. Pick an object to draw – it works well if it is something you've drawn before. Attempt to depict it using your non-dominant hand. It's surprisingly liberating to draw without having any expectations of the finished piece, and to re-experience the act of drawing, which can be taken for granted.

Almeida's work, similarly, makes us reconsider artistic acts, challenging different disciplines at the same time as she works within them. Like Perry and Matisse, Almeida refuses to conform to inherited ideas about what a particular technique or medium is for. By sensing the possibilities of a technique rather than its limits, all of these artists show how fresh and creative ways of making can emerge.

See this:

Helena Almeida, *Drawing (with Pigment)*, 1995–9

Almeida made drawings throughout her career, as a preparatory process, but only started showing them as art in the mid-2000s.

Henri Matisse, *The Snail*, 1953

An illustration of the scale and ambition of Matisse's cut-outs.

Grayson Perry, *Aspects of Myself*, 2001

A self-portrait in pottery, challenging our perceptions about both what art should be and what an artist should be like.

Notes 1. Quoted in Judith Olch Richards (ed.), *Inside the Studio: Two Decades of Talks with Artists in New York* (New York: Independent Curators International, 2004), p.76 2. John Leighton, 'On Photography as a Means or an End', *Journal of the Photographic Society of London*, No. 1, 1 March 1853, p.74 3. Quoted in Helen Little, *Hockney*, Tate Introductions (London: Tate Publishing, 2017), p.25 4. Quoted in *David Hockney: A Retrospective* (Los Angeles, CA: Los Angeles County Museum of Art; London: Thames & Hudson, 1988), p.83 5. Quoted in Wendy Jones, *Grayson Perry: Portrait of the Artist as a Young Girl* (London: Vintage, 2007), p.193 6. Quoted in Jacky Klein, *Grayson Perry* (London: Thames & Hudson, 2013), p.39 7. Quoted in Jones, p.191 8. Quoted in Sarah Thornton, *33 Artists in 3 Acts* (London: Granta, 2015), p.307 9. Quoted ibid. 10. Quoted in Grayson Perry, *Playing to the Gallery* (London: Penguin Books, 2016), p.122 11. Quoted in *Henri Matisse: exposition du centenaire*, Grand Palais, Avril-Septembre 1970 (France: Réunion des musées nationaux, 1970), p.48 12. Jacqueline Duhême, Juliette Rizzi and Flavia Frigeri. 'It Was Like Drawing, but with Scissors...There Was Sensuality in the Cutting'. https://www.tate. org.uk/context-comment/articles/it-was-drawing-scissors-there-was-sensuality-cutting <Summer 2014 (accessed 26 September 2018)> 13. Quoted in *Helena Almeida: Inside Me* (Cambridge: Kettle's Yard, 2009), p.11

DON'T

FORGET

YOURSELF

SONIA BOYCE
MONA HATOUM
CAROLEE SCHNEEMANN

The world is full of creative possibilities to explore. While inspiration can be found by venturing out, don't neglect something a little closer to home. ✱ There's a wealth of source material readily accessible to you – and that's you. Using yourself – your body, your story, your history – puts inspiration, sometimes literally, at your fingertips. You have experiences to share, stories to explore, things that make you uniquely you.

While you can directly inspire your work, your work doesn't have to be directly about you – the artists in this section all use the specific to explore the general. Use the personal to interrogate, speculate or subvert expectations – or all of the above. When you use yourself, you're the one in control.

✱ ⟶ KEEP ON MOVING (see p.66)

USE YOUR BODY

Begin in a basic, but surprisingly frequently overlooked way – with your body. Carolee Schneemann encourages us to think of the parts of the body as 'potential units of movement: face, fingers, hands, toes, feet, arms, legs'.[1] When Schneemann started working in the early 1960s, her use of the body was radical. In *Eye Body: 36 Transformative Actions* (1963), a series of actions carried out in private but documented through photographs, she covered her naked body in 'paint, grease, chalk, ropes, plastic' and stated her intention to establish her 'body as visual territory'.[2] 'Not only am I an image maker,' she said, 'but I explore the image values of flesh as material I choose to work with.'[3] Schneemann used her body to challenge the idea of the heroic male artist. In the first performance of *Interior Scroll* (1975), she read from a scroll she unfurled from her vagina. Its text recounts a conversation with a filmmaker who refused to watch Schneemann's work, criticising her use of traditionally 'feminine' intuition, feeling and bodily processes instead of traditionally 'male' ideas of rational order. Schneemann made her body into a site for creativity, rather than trying to conform to predominantly masculine ideas about what art should be. She used her body to suggest alternative ways to create.

Part of the appeal of performance for Schneemann was that it is a way of making art that is hard to commodify or sell. Basing your work on your body is an inexpensive and accessible way to make art. Your body is capable of many wonderful things: use it.

. . . .

UNDER YOUR THUMB

Your fingerprint is as unique as you are. Use it to make art. Look up the work of artist Judith Ann Braun, who creates huge landscapes using her fingertips. Like Braun, you could use charcoal to make images, or paint, as you would have done as a child. Lay out, or pin up, a large sheet of paper. Put the hand that you aren't using behind your back, and move your other hand to create an image on the paper surface. Try as many techniques as you can think of: press down, trail your fingertips, leave a light imprint of your thumb on the paper. Get to know everything that your tool – your hand – might be able to do.

. . . .

REFRAME YOUR STORY

Your body is part of your way of experiencing the world. Multimedia artist Mona Hatoum's earliest work was made as a 'reaction to this kind of feeling that people were so disembodied around me, people were just like walking intellects and not really giving any attention to the body and the fact that this is part of one's existence'.[4] While Schneemann's body is present and visible in her work, Hatoum's is notable for its seeming absence. She creates work using 'waste' body parts, as in the installation *Recollection* (1995), which features hundreds of hairballs and a weaving on a loom, all made using Hatoum's own dead and discarded hair.

The sense of loss runs through Hatoum's work, influenced by her own biography. Hatoum grew up as a Palestinian living in Lebanon. Visiting Britain in 1975, she found herself forced to remain there after the Lebanese Civil War began. *Measures of Distance* (1988) is one of her most explicitly autobiographical works. In it, the Arabic text of letters sent to Hatoum by her mother while the artist was in exile is layered over images of her mother showering. Rather than their usual role as a bridge between people, the letters here form a barrier between mother and the viewer. This sense of distance is enhanced by the soundtrack, which plays a conversation between the artist and her mother, cut with Hatoum reading English translations of the letters. This is a specific story, but its message is general, speaking, in Hatoum's words, of 'exile, displacement, disorientation and a tremendous sense of loss as a result of the separation caused by war'.[5] Hatoum doesn't use the work to moralise or 'make a direct political statement'.[6] While the issues that she explores have links to her own story, Hatoum deliberately refines them, spending time 'trying to remove the content', so that interpretation won't become limited to the facts of her biography.[7] She uses her personal experience as a way to address larger themes.

REVEAL YOURSELF

★
⟶
COLLECT, RECOLLECT (see p.48)

As Schneemann's example shows, placing yourself in your work can be an act of defiance. In her work *From Tarzan to Rambo: English Born 'Native' Considers her Relationship to the Constructed/Self Image and her Roots in Reconstruction* (1987) (see pages 110–11), Sonia Boyce uses herself to ask questions about society's attitude to black women. Like that of Eduardo Paolozzi, Boyce's photo-based work makes use of mass-produced imagery collected by the artist, such as *Rupert Bear* comics from the 1920s, and *Terrifying Tales* from the 1950s. ★ Boyce, however, places herself alongside these images – she appears 12 times in the work, within two sets of six portraits taken in a photo booth. The viewer has to consider her, the 'English Born "Native"' of the title, in relation to this found imagery, which includes 'golliwog' heads from *Rupert*, 'natives' from *Terrifying Tales* and *Tarzan*, which shows the white man presiding over an exotic presentation of Africa. This is the material that Boyce grew up with in 1960s and '70s Britain, a time when she felt that 'historical and cultural narratives about the black female subject were quite limited'.[8]

Boyce integrated her image with the collected material, sketching onto her own photo portraits and even echoing a Hollywood trope in her snapshots: the 'image of the black person as mystical in some way or as not fully conscious – under the spell of something – voodoo or something other-worldly'.[9] She has made herself visible to suggest how these cultural 'norms' might impact the individual.

THINK OF ME THIS WAY

Photocopy or print out a selection of pictures of yourself. Cut out the background of your photographs – you'll be creating new backgrounds. You could draw or sketch these, or use found imagery like Sonia Boyce. You could place yourself among things that you remember from your childhood, or perhaps imagine yourself to have in the future. Take yourself to somewhere that you really want to go, and somewhere that you'd rather not. How do you feel you fit in each scenario? How does it change the way that you see yourself?

Boyce uses her own image and memories to make a general statement: 'It was never just about me,' she has said of her early work, 'but, more broadly, about the role and representation of the black female figure.'[10] She knows that the work will provoke a variety of responses, depending on the personal experiences of the viewer. 'I don't know how other black people respond to seeing these connections put together,' she says. 'I'm sure it will be quite painful.'[11] Bringing your individual experience to art directly challenges any idea that there's one way of seeing and approaching the world. Boyce now works mainly on collaborative projects, another way of amplifying different voices within the art world.

Art can express many aspects of yourself: your personal relationships, place in society or, more elementally, your physical body. As these artists show, the personal can be political – a protest or protestation of how you see the world. What aspects of yourself could you take inspiration from to do the same?

See this:

Sonia Boyce, *From Tarzan to Rambo: English Born 'Native' Considers her Relationship to the Constructed/Self Image and her Roots in Reconstruction*, 1987

A self-portrait that integrates photography and found material to register a protest at images of black women in British culture.

Mona Hatoum, *Measures of Distance*, 1988

The artist uses materials from her own life to create a sense of distance and loss that surpasses the specific.

Carolee Schneemann, *Interior Scroll*, 1975

A print documenting Schneemann's performance, which has been brushed and splattered with juice, urine and coffee.

Notes 1. Carolee Schneemann, 'From the Notebooks', 1962–3, in Kristine Stiles and Peter Selz (eds), *Theories and Documents of Contemporary Art: A Sourcebook of Artists' Writings*, 2nd revised and expanded edn (Berkeley, CA: University of California Press, 2012), p.841 2. Carolee Schneemann and Bruce R. McPherson (ed.), *More than Meat Joy: Performance Works and Selected Writings* (Kingston, NY: McPherson & Co., 1997), p.52 3. Ibid. 4. Mona Hatoum, in interview with John Tusa, 2006, in *Stiles and Selz*, 2012, p.675 5. Quoted in Guy Brett, Michael Archer and Catherine de Zegher, *Mona Hatoum* (London: Phaidon Press, 1997), p.140 6. Quoted in Rachel Cooke, 'Mona Hatoum: "It's All Luck. I Feel Things Happen Accidentally"', https://www.theguardian.com/artanddesign/2016/apr/17/mona-hatoum-interview-installation-artist-tate-modern-exhibition <17 April 2016 (accessed 19 September 2018)> 7. Quoted ibid. 8. Quoted in Jennifer Higgie, 'Sonia Boyce: 30 Years of Art and Activism', https://frieze.com/article/sonia-boyce-30-years-art-and-activism <29 May 2018 (accessed 19 September 2018)> 9. Quoted in 'Look Closer: Explore from Tarzan to Rambo', https://www.tate.org.uk/art/artists/sonia-boyce-794/explore-tarzan-rambo, <accessed 19 September 2018> 10. Quoted in Higgie 11. Quoted in 'Sonia Boyce: *From Tarzan to Rambo: English Born "Native" Considers her Relationship to the Constructed/Self Image and her Roots in Reconstruction*', https://www.tate.org.uk/art/artworks/boyce-from-tarzan-to-rambo-english-born-native-considers-her-relationship-to-the-t05021 <accessed 19 September 2018>

ativity

ty Crea

ity Cre

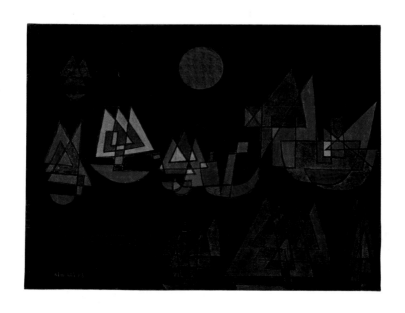

Paul Klee

Ships in the Dark, 1927

Oil paint on canvas

Tacita Dean
Majesty, 2006
Gouache on photograph
mounted on paper

Richard Long
A Line Made by Walking, 1967
Photograph, gelatin silver print
on paper with graphite on board

Paul Cézanne
Montagne Sainte Victoire,
1905–6
Watercolour on paper

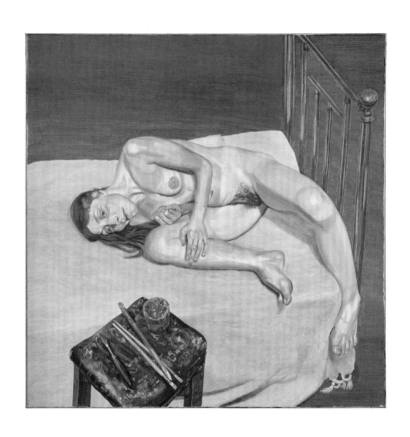

Lucian Freud

Naked Portrait, 1972–3

Oil paint on canvas

Francis Bacon

Study for a Portrait, 1952

Oil paint and sand on canvas

Rebecca Warren
Versailles, **2006**
Clay, polystyrene, steel,
aluminium and wood

Paul Gauguin

Faa Iheihe, 1898

Oil paint on canvas

Sonia Boyce
*From Tarzan to Rambo: English Born 'Native' Considers
her Relationship to the Constructed/Self Image
and her Roots in Reconstruction*, 1987
Black-and-white photographs on paper, photocopies on
paper, acrylic paint, ballpoint pen, crayon and felt-tip pen

Henri Matisse
The Snail, **1953**
Gouache on paper, cut
and pasted on paper
mounted on canvas